As Long as the Sun Shines

Janet Rogers

BookLand
press

Published by BookLand Press
15 Allstate Parkway
Suite 600
Markham, Ontario L3R 5B4
www.booklandpress.com

Printed in Canada

Front cover image © Nancy King

Library and Archives Canada Cataloguing in Publication

Rogers, Janet Marie, 1963-, author
    As long as the sun shines / Janet Rogers.

(Modern indigenous voices)
Poems.
Issued in print and electronic formats.
ISBN 978-1-77231-083-2 (softcover). --ISBN 978-1-77231-084-9 (EPUB).
--ISBN 978-1-77231-085-6 (PDF)

    I. Title. II. Series: Modern indigenous voices

PS8585.O395158A92 2018   C811'.6   C2018-903722-9
                                                 C2018-903723-7

We acknowledge the support of the Canada Council for the Arts, which last year invested $153 million to bring the arts to Canadians throughout the country. We acknowledge the support of the Ontario Arts Council (OAC), an agency of the Government of Ontario. We acknowledge the financial support of the Ontario Media Development Corporation for our publishing activities.

Table of Contents

Nations March Together

The Ever Present Tomahawk | 11

Well Educated Guesses | 14

Indian Now | 16

Know Your Generosity | 17

Dream Games | 20

Face(less) | 21

Stories from the Vault | 23

Usufruct | 26

Klee Wyck Woman | 27

Confederation 150 | 30

Title Me This | 33

Janvier | 36

Bank-notable E. Pauline | 38

Louise Bernice | 41

Big Strong Stable and Tall | 44

White Indian Academic Wannabe Expert | 45

2017 Indian | 47

Proof of Power

Revenge is Honest | 53

Allegations | 56

Choose Your Side | 58

Scram-bled Words | 61

Cigar Poems | 63

Reading Cards | 67

Candle Light Inspirations | 70

Change | 73

Coming Back | 74

Addicted | 75

Six O'clock | 78

Strong Dark Coffee | 80

NDNs on the Airwaves | 81

Faces | 84

Singing the Peace Hymn

Ocean and Shore | 89

Belly of the Mother | 90

The London Cocktail | 93

Hot Oceans | 95

Suspended | 96

Croxxing | 98

Salt of the Land | 99

House of Stories | 102

Into out of the Woods | 104

Born (Again) Savage | 108

A Bullet You Can't Call Back | 109

No Place | 111

No More Birthdays | 112

Good Trades | 113

Far Away Fires | 115

Foreword

The book title, *As Long as the Sun Shines*, references the concept of forever. This is associated with the Haudenosaunee Two Row Wampum Agreement: an eloquent, succinct and thoughtful agreement based on relationship management and environmental concern initiated 400 years ago. As a poet and as a Haudenosaunee woman, I am drawn to root my poetic practices in my culture while addressing the myriad of subjects that have provided inspiration for this collection of poems.

I pay honour and give thanks to the numerous residencies where these poems had time and a place to find their way to the page, and be assembled into three distinct sections: Nations March Together, Proof of Power and Singing the Peace Hymn. Nia:wen, thank you to the Eastern Comma Writer-in-Residence program in Cambridge, Ontario hosted by RARE and Musagetes, to the Indigenous Artist-in-Residence program in Blairmore, Alberta hosted by the University of Lethbridge, Alberta, to the Historic Joy Kogawa House Writer-in-Residence program in Vancouver, British Columbia, and to the Artist-in-Residence program hosted by the Institute of American Indian Arts and the Sunrise Springs Resort in Santa Fe, New Mexico.

All of the residency locations enlightened the writing found in this collection and as such, I had the opportunity to replicate the role of the storytellers of old who travelled beyond their communities to offer colourful orations for the benefit of all.

BookLand Press' *Modern Indigenous Voices* book series has published many great talents of our time and I am so pleased and honoured to be part of this collection which is dedicated exclusively to publishing and promoting contemporary Indigenous voices along with BookLand's commitment to translating each book within the series into the author's Indigenous language. I very much look forward to the Mohawk translation of this collection by Mohawk speaker Jeremy Green being released by BookLand Press in 2019. To the best of our knowledge, a Mohawk language poetry book does not currently exist and we are thrilled to provide a language resource to ensure the preservation and intergenerational transmission of the Mohawk language to future generations.

As Long as the Sun Shines is my sixth published poetry collection. It is offered to readers as a contemporary time marker from a distinct Indigenous perspective utilizing rhythm, rhyme, experimental and list poetry as well as oratory for the page. These poems are a journey, traversing time, place and people – three important pieces of the storyteller's puzzle.

From my heart to yours, enjoy.

~ Janet Rogers

Nations March Together

The Ever Present Tomahawk

statue buzz
is dismantling
power structures
as we reposition ourselves
reframe greatness
in metal and stone
it's about control

their story tellers'
language is limited
choosing the most accessible
superficial recognizable
as perpetrator or hyper-villain
only sexualized Indigenous women
need apply

white-washed replicas
of warrior archetypes
chiseled with immigrant aesthetic
accentuate the hyper masculine
put a bird on his head
put a tomahawk in his hand

if the two row law
is really about harmony
then we will line our rivers
with icons of ourselves
so onlookers can marvel
from over there
we will immortalize our women
clan creatures and land
personify it all and leave it nameless

our weapons were never activated
without intelligent considerations
the un-sheathed blade and oversized war club
looks like law degrees
bids for seats in the senate
the new warrior fights you
with your own weapons
thanks for the education
this is not puppetry
but clever strategy

colonial gaze embraces
sexualized squaws
cure-alls and mascots
angry protestors
addicts and tax burdens
rebellious and subversive
a dismal dying race

generosity offers
wise old Indians
interpreters of dreams
fishing guides
pipe carrying medicine men
givers of names
givers of feathers
traditional story tellers
costumed clad entertainers

what do you remember
Oka warrior and SQ
forever seared into view
are you a good Indian
or a big bad savage

this binary leaves little room
for me or you
statues are publicly funded
emblems of inequality
set in stone

Indians that serve the white man
get remembered and immortalized
get books written about them
the contentious ones get time
get copied and told to be quiet
we are found in toy stores so they can
play out their narratives of us

put a headdress on it
make them shake hands

we continue to be captured
as award winning novels
reporters entering enemy territories
just to get the story

take a mental snapshot of this
Indian poet, shoulders square
feet flat on the floor
pandering to no one
liberated and deliberate
reciting original verses
in control

Well Educated Guesses

the body holds memories
documented in the heart
no treaty law
no tax returns
no reimbursement upon proof
we haven't earned the right
to see it
and yet there it is
multi-generational weak
and reproduced
labelled in triplicate
irregardless
of relationship
I am not a file
I am representing
the triumphs
and unfortunate choices
making friends of them
only to save a fraction
of what was already ours
we are left with apology exhaustion
and heat-stroke headaches

if I refuse to sign the census
do I disappear
is my memory erased
does the imprint of my shadow
upon the many lands I have travelled
sink into collected layers
where the future has no recourse
but to reinvent itself from well educated guesses
will I become a digital elder

reliant on electrical power
my caption will read
I've seen it all and still know nothing

if man is the measure of all things
then lets bury the ruler
along with other knowledge
we managed to keep from
the museum curator
they have no moral jurisdiction
over my body, or my mother's

inviting understanding
is opening a door
that can never be closed again
examination of who we were
meant to be
has no other option
but to operate from speculation
it's not the immigrants
but those who think
they're not immigrants
identity morphs into opinion
I stand, contrary to personal safety
and allow you to stare
while I shift directions
leave you to ponder vacated spaces
of where I once was
for if I am to become an object
for your cultural authority
at lease allow me to
print the labels
where nothing is lost
to interpretation

Indian Now

giving over power
tweeting is not speaking
trusting technology with longevity
I am writing on scraps of paper
by hand in cursive
poetry by popularity
soundbites and whatever makes you famous
attention span captured
in limited characters
abbreviated phrases
misunderstood meanings
dissected and rejected friendships
I am asking the internet
for teachings
because I want to be Indian NOW
want the right to wear moccasins and earrings
have permission to tell others
you can't, that's racist

I pack paper poems
carry the weight of these words
into tomorrow
don't click
don't click-click
don't click it away
this is cyber-reality
our ancestors saw coming
the spirit of your convictions
is all that will be left of you

Know Your Generosity

discipline is a path chosen
feet on the ground at all times
brings you to water bodies
where motivations activate
family is no mistake
this work, this life, this life, is work

pay attention to moments of grace

know what you want to serve
we have control of our thoughts
and actions
we open our hands
to hold the whole world at once

create opportunities to love
know, who you love

build a memory bank of limitless happiness
prayer feelings is feeling the prayer feelings
running around with laughter
keep feeling
good

notice beauty

we are natural in the Indian way
we hold love as holy
it feels good to pray

embrace woman power

it is now, not the future
it is an old way
changing everything
showing men how to be beautiful too
rejecting teachings exclusive to them
we awake together
this is the future
now

know your conscientiousness
be aware of what you are aware of
keep it alive in timelessness
this is not an instructional
but a list from them who have gone before
not dead but evolved
call them grandmothers
who are your grandmothers
look and see what they spill
from the cup
it is yours

know your gifts
know your generosity

Creation energy
bring us together
turn it upside down, reverse it
don't believe in it too hard
and never believe but think
keep the portals open to source
feel what's true for you

learn by ear

listen like you are by the fire
like you are part of the circle
knowing your turn is coming
telling stories of self
own your own story
it doesn't belong to anyone else

make curiosity your passion

keep looking
there is always more happiness
more of the mystery
more tragedies
that make us firm
we are born from inspiration
so be inspired
and pay it forward

sing your medicine songs

be a radio even though no one is tuned in
someone will find your dial
someone will turn up the volume
the land is always listening
your wordless song is a miracle
know your courage

Dream Games

atoning in the truest of times
entrusting and recounting
listening to my brother
recovering himself
with Elder help
spirit parents adopting him
offering Blackfoot ways
they say
shed dead skin no longer needed
they lift his chin
buried far too long
they protect him
from all directions
he stands on their lands
learning who he is again
who he is meant to be again

returning to himself
and receiving family love
always ready for him
he is returning
from another vision of non-tradition
his gaze extended along horizons
he carries with him
a wife and beautiful girl
a parental lineage he perpetuates
recreates dreamlike visions
spins them from sacred conceptions
remembers to ask questions
knowing the culture he creates
comes with weight
he is brother Bear
ready

Face(less)

young woman
never thinking
of reflection
her purpose to serve
the people
healer of hopelessness
passing a pond
catching her likeness
caught by attractiveness
seen for the first time
her own beauty
birthing ego
looking
unable to look away
stayed all day
fascinated
dark full eyes
looking back at
earth tone skin
flawless cheeks like spring moons
a rosebud of a mouth
soft button of a nose
that neck her throat
shoulders statuesque
captivated, never tiring of her own portrait
this wicked consumption
sickness spreading quick

her fate
punishment severe
forsaking her people
suffering in her absence
disturbing unnatural

faceless forever
plainness
reminders
to stay the course
cruel punishments
our specialness
supersedes superficialness
this faceless one
decorates and entertains
she stands as cornhusk woman
in stories, teachings and games

Stories from the Vault

Indigenous Kiss started it all
fresh it was called
it didn't take long
to want to
wash their hands of it
assigned someone
to write the obit
our rich histories
brimming with story
they wanted to stop collecting
and call it a day

the murals are still missing
Carl Beam's broken mould in the
North American Iceberg
holds more knowledge than
the library of congress
these links to tradition
are sacred medicine
and the men who protected them
warriors all the same

"Steal our Land,
Steal our Children
Steal our Art too"
offered three hundred measly dollars
for your mother's breast
for your brother's heart
Norval flew down from the Astral plane
dragging a bargain bin behind him
cultural crimes perpetrated
mis-labelled treasures
sit in musty graves

this is not a dumping ground
but bodies that talk
sometimes in deep whispers
others in spirit voice
Jane Ash, Up All Night Girl
and Skeleton Shaman
the greatest discussions happen
behind the canvas
sub-stories, gossip
opinions and jokes
the eastern ones
holding up the western ones
circles of support
and sometimes there's consensus
at least we can all agree
a national gallery
is long overdue
and not too much
to ask for
do you?

art prison
is this where the great ones go
when it took so long for our voices
to take shape
for them to validate
is the museum the best
we can offer the foundation
of all cultural definition
take them off the office wall
before I steal them

activate
with movement and momentum
stand back and let these things breathe
the artist quotes two prices

one for kin one for admin
parameters around government funds
considered peculiar
implements negative influences
on the curator
he with the ruler and wristwatch
a balancing act of nationhood
and compliance

look with intellectual lens
catalogue it all
before they're all gone
and a new lexicon
takes hold to describe the work

Usufruct

Salish painter stands
back against canvass
wings stretched to the edges
proclaims
All this is mine

Salish painter states
kings and queens
from distant lands
want to rule his forests
his waters his blue skies
controlled by greedy gods
parliament represents one percent
with no spiritual teachings other than
obey - okay

the people say
This is not working
not willing to reduce consumption
or consider alter-natives
anthems sung
to jack-hammer sounds
we are the trees
standing in resistance
we are usufucked Indians
you see
okay

Klee Wyck Woman

her enormity
sat mouse-like quiet
a paradox of celebrity
and misdirected distain
she was a woman wanting
to find herself
inside fascinating landscapes
she was the gaze
respectfully reflecting
not taking away or manipulating
but inventing a style
for a spirit satisfied
Blunden
breathing in
cedar-spiced oxygen
hearing language
dampened by man
verses in pigments
poetry in colour
sounds of universal truths
inside Indian Church
amplifying the sacred
something not offered
by humans
Klee Wyck Woman
chooses a gypsy's life
creating mysteries
in search of
exquisite silence
the sacred symphony

making secret agreements
and last chance proposals
drafting pacts and promises
where everyone wins
rejecting glamorous interpretations
conveying from her own soul
her true purpose
it was worth it
perceived sacrifices
not sacrifice at all
but massive investments
defending dark canvases
from a small world
of short-sighted critics
a decisive individual
supported but not dependent
on what others thought
the ground work she laid
resolute decisions made
new territory for
the north american women
to consider for themselves
instinctively knowing
there'd be more and more
to grow this sisterhood of
painters, singers, poets and carvers
but the territories she could not save
she preserved for future view
we can see what she saw
in Kispiox
and that
now gone

she who lost and found herself
by giving over ego
the nature the people
the originals who named her
Laughing One
a respectful giggle
echoes in the distance
pleased by visitors
curious and a bit embarrassed
by it all

Confederation 150

ah canada
standing defiantly behind a line
that doesn't quite protect or define
as it was wished
and won by war
these spoils are yours
so what can you claim?
with flimsy parchment that proclaims
ownership citizenship
a severely superficialness
taking and overtaking
the dismissing and denying
buried under layers
the ice is petrifying
offering hard rock shields
labeled canadian
a nationalistic resource
where nothing cultivates
and nothing to trade
did you think
the steel staples
would hold it together
did you remember
to ask permissions
or make paper consultations
using the queen's english
ah canada
do not slip me the tongue
and call it a french kiss
how do two languages survive 65 or more?
an agenda of insults with your
ideas of colonial distinction
pretty little tricks in lyrics

sung from the immigrant's hearts
your crests in cloth tells all
as two red nations
stand divided either side
a dying maple leaf
a thinly penciled treaty
and centred symbol almost stable
until autumn's justice sucks the truth from it
and we begin again.

offerings in song
to join in false chorus
another choice to remain forgetful
but your soldiers stay true
and their patriot hearts
continue to glow with pride
while we the originals write our own journals
after disrupted chapters leaving my people to
fight, flee or die
the strength of our identity
was formed before you
were even born
and doesn't include hops and hockey
who are you, exactly?
listening to the mother corp
with terrestrial signals
mining stories and rewriting ours
your race hate-filled comments
take this country's temperature and count its votes
so listen close
there is no home if there is no native land
sing about it all you want
the harmonies will always
be off key to me
and the Chief reciting
his lament 50 years previous

said it all from the west
ah canada
how many of me
had to die so you can be you
reconcile is not something you read about
it's something you do

Title Me This

The Generous Book Titles

The New People
The Eskimo People
Children of the People
People of the First Man
The Sun Dance People
People of the River
Our Ancient People
The People of the Centre
The Crow People
People of the Dessert
The Fourth World People

Plain Ol' Indian Book Titles

Indian Primitive
Indian Affairs in Colonial New York
The Indian Traders
The Indian and His Problems
Held Captive by Indians
Fighting Indians of the West
Buried Indians
Western Indians
The Indians of Texas
The Texas Indians
The White Man's Indian
The Southern Indians
Indian Running
An Incredible Indian
The Soul of the Indian
The Crow Indians

The Indian Man
America's Indian
Indian Country
American Indian Women
The Urban Indian

Man Book Titles

Old Man Coyote
Paper Medicine Man
Ancient Men
The Naked Man
He Who Always Wins

Woman Book Titles

White Wolf Woman
Daughters of the Dessert
Native American Woman
Medicine Woman

American Book Titles

The Savages of America
The Tortured Americans
American Indian Crisis
American Indian Trickster
The First Americans

Red Book Titles

The Rhythm of the Redman
Red Skins, Ruffled Shirts and Red Necks
Red Chiefs and White Challengers
In Red Man's Land
Red Brethren

Objects of Bright Pride
And Still the Waters Run
The Buffalo Hunters
Lost Labourers
Children of Coyote
The Prophets of the Earth
Dancing Gods
Voices of the Winds
The Corn Goddess
Our Brothers' Keeper
All Our Relations
The Primal Mind
Peyote Cult
Healers of the Mountain
Shadow Catchers
Dwellers at the Source
The Dancing Healer
People of the Deer
Forgotten Founders
Sun Chiefs
Hunters of the North Forest
Dreamers Without Power
Magic Dwellers
Wind Chanters of Sky and Earth
Warrior Apache
Cherokee Cavalier
Disinherited
The Wind is my Mother
Warriors Without Weapons
Visions of a Vanishing Race
Stone Faces
Lost Tribes of Sunken Continents
Word Dancers
Breeds and Half Breeds
Lost Empires of Living Tribes

Janvier

he reaches deep
into earth's core
pulls out imploded worlds
evoking sounds
technicolour clouds
where reflections
recognizable and obscure
share the same sky
he captures pow wow creatures
hangs them with a hunter's pride
not as game trophies
but emblems of beauty
his heart beats with culture
Janvier's inclusive colours
make directionless maps
turned left, rotated right
leading to middle and out again
every time
grounded foundational
brush-touched wisps
whispers of Blue Quill on canvas
volumes of truth
curator's call it evidence
his visual language
surprises of the recognizable
his landscapes
resonate like drum beats
confronting and combining
pain and territory
investigating ground memories

"We are the land, and the land is us"

reclaimed his name
and threw the digits away
287 never signed again
young women bragging
about sharing a meal with him
a friend said he helped him
I am afraid to approach
too close with pen
that could leap from my
anxious hand to mismark
his perfect imperfections

cross-hatching
and slash-hatching
soon you be sky diving
from flat surfaces
landing on 3-D dimensions

worlds and drums and moons
and planets and stars and bodies
and hearts and lungs
multiple microscope lenses
cross-sections of our selves
lives disease free and vital
pulsating at different frequencies
living as they never expected him

Eagle song, he calls it
Red Skin, Eleven Old Men
October Sun, A Gift From Above
Neo-Red Power, I Remember
35 Drums playing, This Proof of Life
this proof of power

Bank-notable E. Pauline

(in response to poet E. Pauline Johnson
making the short list of women considered)

have you seen her iconic profile
with bear claw necklace
gifted her by a writer, admirer
soft features and youthful gaze
looking sideways
towards a future unknown

we don't vote
we have our own
councils and culture
our own governance and authority
we still engage through currency
and why shouldn't we further exchange
in dollar bills decorated with the face
of this beautiful brown poet

many may not know it
but she traversed these territories
nineteen times across much more rugged terrain
landscapes inspired her pen
early trains carried her in
small cities and more remote places
she took to on foot

all the trouble made
for the love of poetry and stage
but also for a chance to say
what she saw
and what she saw
was natural magnificence
and injustices, man-made

should Pauline be featured on our legal tender?
I'd say so and it best to be a sawbuck or more
for we are all passing through
processing a current state of reconciliation
making our way to the other side
this paper currency will survive
long after we get forgotten

so who else should be there
overseeing the original relationship
Double Wampum – Tekahionwake
we call it wistah, shiny silver things
or Ojistoh – like the white stars
her chieftain father and english mother
made this star for us to claim
a legacy large enough
for poetry, writing identity
untamed

we have good reason to celebrate her
and place this lady on our notes
with every transaction
she'll be there
reminding us
remember
remember how we got here
what it took to survive

she will speak to us
of the original glory
from an unprecedented
and permanent place
important for young women
wondering
what mark can I make?

they will see a sister
151 years after confederacy
a territory we can all share
yes Pauline
your gifts and purpose
still serve us today
rooted in these massive lands
of that we cannot deny

Louise Bernice

it isn't opinion
or historical fact
but lived experience
spoken from a woman
who keeps it personal
pens portraits of family
reclaiming, rescuing herself from the fires
before Burning in her Midnight Dream

her eyes bright and clear
brimming with wisdom
a healthy dose of fight behind them
for the right to live with dignity
so we can all live with dignity
she leads us and heals us
from massive acts of human violations
to culture and self

Cree Gregory, a contemporary
thrilled that another
had the guts to write
in the language unapologetically
he, a hungry puppy sopping up her poetry
like mid-night meals Auntie served
between beads and stories

what do we call poems that call us home
does it matter?
as long as that train keeps rolling
miles of tracks filled with laughter
struggle and quiet contemplation

she did this work
she rode the rails
she waits for the rest of us
to join her at the station

in the minds-eye she is silver
the kind Indian women take out
on special occasions
Sky Dancer is her astral configuration
shine she says
burn the whole thing down
wash your face in the ashes
of what used to be
remember who you are
always speak your truth
there is no excuse not to

her name is poetry
Louise Bernice
we gather at her feet
hungry for teachings and written permissions
we listen to raw sex stories absent of romance
skin as hunting tents
comparing healers to dreamers
lawyers of our ways
negotiate and navigate
woman pathways

She is *Crooked Good*
her cathartic verses drenched
in zero degree separation
the vatican receiving packages
full of Sky Dancer's confessions
pieces of her mind hit the queen's door
like a rolled up newspaper
she's baffled them all

her bright spirit pierced by Blue Quills
survivor of state-sanctioned abduction
keeps her language frozen
inside Bear Bones and Feathers
learned to write through
perfecting suicide notes
confused youth with nowhere safe
so everything became an act of preservation

gorgeous alchemist
of high-bred 3rd official language
a delicious mix of Cree/English
and we are back at her table
feasting with our eyes on words
that mean so much more than
their english translation
this is why we hang around
our winter-haired Mama
for offerings so much more
than any other

Big Strong Stable and Tall

be my ono^gwa^a (stalk)
big strong stable and tall
we are connected by our ok'te'a (roots)
so why not bring our onyo'nia (husks)
together and make sweet corn love
a love so good it makes our odio^sa (leaves) shake
makes o'gio^t (silk) of our rough skins
we nibble on each others' o'nis'ta (kernels)
offer your ono^gwa^a (cob) to me
I'll dangle my oji'jut (tassles) over you
run through fall fields and harvest what is ours

White Indian Academic Wannabe Expert

did I lead you astray
did I say I was something
from what I actually am
never claimed to be
the expert Indian
didn't get a degree
in Indigenous celebrity
instant recognition
before community claims me
I operate from a global foundation
carrying home as passport
and compass back

did I mislead you
or did you think
by getting an institutional
Indian name
you can tell me
what all this is
where it all comes from
how I am
doing it wrong
you five-minute Indian
taking your tiny pouch
of teaching
going up against
my fifty-five years
of walking in this skin
rooting through
confusion of others
is my education

you fucking career-almost-Indian
just stop playing
with this culture
outsider anthropologist
pimping pain and struggles
as award winning novels
penned from the deluxe comfort
of your convention
writing about my realities
speaking with authority
for me and mine
the more you rise
the more we morph
warped academic rewards
with built in audience
posturing is posing
you goddamn Grey Owl
where were you
when we stood
legs shaking
on the front lines
on top of the waters
pulling with all our might
maintaining a way of life
face to face
with authority
holding integrity
where the hell
were you then?

2017 Indian

The, Reconciliation, Indian

The, Happy Canada 150, Indian

The, you gotta be kidding me, Indian

The, land acknowledgement vs. land repatriation, Indian

The, dancing bear, now pay me, Indian

The, pissed off can't wait for 2018, Indian

The, head on swivel, confused as fuck, Indian

The, 150 grant writing, Indian

The, reconciliation pet, Indian

The, Canadian Aboriginal, Indian

The, sliding down your sacred mountain into a great big fat paycheque, Indian

The, hand-to-mouth front-line rejecting government funds, Indian

The, marry-out stay-out, Indian

The, barely native taking up a lot of space, Indian

The, pandering to the white-man, Indian

The, returning home, Indian

The, CBC go-to, Indian

The, anxious for the future due to losing great leaders like Arthur Manuel, Leonard George but not Dennis Banks, Indian

The, culturally exploitive, Indian

The, getting visited by the PM in a tipi on parliament hill, Indian

The, red carpet, Indian

The, working poor, Indian

The, bodies in the river, Indian

The, learning languages online, Indians

The, surviving the streets Indians

The, assaulted in canadian tire no justice, Indians

The, Elders shaking their heads that this is all happening again, Indians

The, burning the flag on the railroad, Indians

The, smart but never get elected, Indians

The, walking with water, Indians

The, running for justice, Indians

The, military combat trained, Indians

The, still in love, Indians

The, old school listening to Red Bone, Indians

The, fluent, Indians

The, bougie colonized, Indians

The, beautiful regalia wearing, Indians

The, university degree, Indians

The, walking in two worlds, Indians

The, apology exhausted, Indians

The, fed up with the MMIW Inquiry, Indians

The, farming their own lands, Indians

The, fighting on twitter, Indians

The, ceremony for hire, Indians

The, real thing, Indians

The, ball-breaking and barrier busting, Indians

The, skirt shaming, Indians

The, two-spirit burning down closets, Indians

The, raised fist photo op, Indian

The, under paid under appreciated artist, Indian

The, finally getting some recognition, Indian

The, not reliant on colonial approval, Indian

The, don't call me Indian, Indians

The, making trades, Indians

The, writing other peoples' stories, Indians

The, vocal, not shutting up, Indians

The, butchering that elk, Indians

The, moose hide square wearing, not doing much about ending violence against women, but getting a ton of resource extraction money to make a website, Indians

The, low profile, wise, Indian

The, pan-Indian

The, yoga, reiki, meditation, Indian

The, don't talk to me, don't touch me, Indian

The, John Trudell, Indian

The, pow wow, Indian

The, no fixed address so just pay me in cash, Indian

Proof of Power

Revenge is Honest

revenge is honest
while its ugly cousin regret
sits silent
and the thing
you promised
was broken
before it even
left your mouth

I lived with suspicions
like racoons hiding
in the attic
the waiting became torturous
why didn't you, why didn't you
why didn't you
just say it

you couldn't see I was bleeding
leaving a trail of clues
leading straight to my open wounds
this ass is yours
these hips skip
to your lou my darling
you've got me
bent over, broken
chocking down feelings
in the big wet kisses of another
I am ruined
you've screwed it
I am left wrecked
and wanting

remember me, wild!
I didn't mind the constraints
as long as you were the one
enforcing them
I didn't mind being distracted
with fantasy
all the live long day

but your apology lost its melody
and my ability to suspend disbelief
landed heavy as a wrecking ball
on the walls of a house
made of clay
why didn't you, why didn't you
why didn't you
just say it?
silence is regret

I played the fool
only for you
only when I wanted to
consumed with what I used to do for you
crisp! your collar
pinch! your ears
coo to you as a newborn
feed you like a baby bird

we both shook the soda bottle
you were so eager to pop the top
while I did my damnedest
to keep it from bursting
neither of us winning
we are still chasing
the prize

in the end
your Mama took you in
and I turned to family too
an unsatisfying truce
reviewing all the things
I'll never do for you again
heal you with these hands
wear your favourite perfume
defend your inabilities
listen to your goddamn poetry

too many hard hard lessons
never left me
wiser or stronger
instead
I am haunted by a love
that by rights
should have seen
time's touch on flesh
the ultimate sunset

this love was nothing
but a long musical interlude
made of repeated licks
interrupted harmonies
that could have carried us
back to stars

as consolation
you said
regret is for suckers
in passing
I replied
but revenge is honest

Allegations

there is something
in the word allegations
that says
I don't believe you
you have to convince me
give me reason
to convict them
I can't hear you

when

all's I got is a story
of a vomitus experience
there aren't enough showers
they keep doing it to others
everybody knows this
can't understand
the drive inside them
volatile and venomous
toxic and constant
like stealing my culture
just to wind me up
she
is Ghomeshi
and Duncan Campbell Scott
she
wants to whip it out
just to show you who's boss

filing *"allegations"*
responding to questions
incident reports and severity scores
name the players
assign the numbers
discrimination
we know is being perpetrated
many times over
for far too long
taking aim and shooting
racking up victims
not about blame
but protecting
not me, but us all
anyone demonstrating
something of value
and exuberance
she will shoot
harassment
vats of it
ego so fragile
feeding on the illogical

enough now
we've all had
enough now

that's my
official statement

Choose Your Side

coward come hero
tough enough to shoot blind
into the back of the head
forcing the courts
to tell his lie

murderer settler
smoking gun in his acquitted hand
he didn't mean it
he didn't intend
to take the weapon
pregnant with three bullets
he didn't regret
or recount with remorse
aiming his angry dick
at point-blank range
killing, killing, killing
again
killing, killing, killing
again

this pigskin farmer
playing out colonizer's
true fantasy
eradication like vermin
he, believing rotten education
brainwashed robot
unthinking
he didn't reach
expected levels of evolution
bastard courts, protection
of their own

no questions no confrontation
a sleeping man/boy
loved and expected home
food waited upon his arrival
a spirit dish now served

canadians
in all their ignorance
and denial as immigrants
rally for their murdering hero
with monetary contributions
expose what they've been holding
in their glowing hearts all along
ridiculous notions of reconciliation
they hate us

is it really about land?

because I was there
occupying the same
emotional territory
with family, angry
shocked, not shocked
overwhelmed and simultaneously
deflated

take your laws
and shove them
up your rotting
stinking, racist
land stealing
white supremacist
hate breeding
colonial ass

eye for an eye justice
recorded as Great Law
choose your side
and be quick about it
before this history
repeats itself
again

Scram-bled Words

sewn felts save
refer rave

farer fava
power beer

koper wear
we-berp-pork

ho-hire-fech
lemony-moi

mom-loin-yen
silk loks
sekl

IOU soonr
or-ruins on-so

U R nois-oo
vliner-exd

need-liver
lexinr vid

diner-vex-il
rexn-livd

wi-wilos-doe
lie-lowds-si

disil-lowe
owi wisl-led

pie-peece-sex
se-speech ex-hi

except-tise
sec-sieze pex

ay-roofe
royo-ref-ay

leupee-sol
up poleese
pule lees

Cigar Poems

1.

stay inside
the muse is saying
listen for coins clicking
that is your cue
to go forward
only then can you
break the seal of your winter door
notice what the season is saying
for you

recovery reveals all things
your fortune has grown
delivering wings
don't worry if numbers don't line up
take risks that come with individuality
remember you are number five
your cycles repeats after nine
your questions are part of the process

see the mountains?
walk towards them
let your cautious steps
translate respect

2.

they call you Warrior
they say you inspire
this is their choice
you have no say

lovers wait
for decay of yesterday
to leave in peace
contentment is greater
than happiness in the hand
telling you, you can't stay

together music is made
from familiar phrases
it pleases the winds
when things change

just because
we have tapped cups
does not mean we are done
togetherness grows
in ways wild of containment
it's okay

embrace emotions
left over from age
it is not loss we face
but experience gained
they call you Warrior
today

3.

taking a stand
is risk turned in
on itself
gambling
with reputations
seeing yourself
from opposite angles
is that your question
we can see
yesterday for the story it is
it forces us to spend less time
worrying
these teachings, I told you

I reach
with one hand
and save the other
for friendship
steady celebrations
relationships
and foolhardy feasts

this is my heart
hold it
just for a bit

one rotation around the sun
takes longer than a book
to be made
I laugh at bare-breasted promises
no more important than
a casual handshake

4.

I want smoke
I want the sky
desire of both
lives together in spaces
human, in earthly time

when the match is struck
it makes a sound similar
to a sneeze
the house shifts
in high winds
it wants to come in
this is Saturday

I want the stars
I want my language

I am exhausted
I know what
this age feels like
so I can tell you
what it feels like
for me

the locals say
it gets wicked
and there is plenty more
on the way
I look to the highway
envy those leaving

keep candles handy
everything is creaking
it is speaking the language
of union collisions

Reading Cards

1.

you have good fortune
walk with it
never discard it
it is yours
use it

change
may come
with a healthy dose
of nervous suspicion
remember
the universe has you
remember
stay out of its way
say thank you

this could be nothing more
than poetry preach'n
but it has come to my attention
come to my attention
attention

a loving union
takes time and observation
you will get help
but not as expected
be willing to release
ways that no longer serve
light and sound
necessary in the middle
of winter

2.

you have grown into yourself
your breath leaves your chest
in celebration of another year
the stars are witness to your fall
they watch as you recover
and carry on

your choices get better
fortune starts to follow
stay courageous
include others
every time you spin the wheel
their fate is directly effected
you are reflected in their choices too
they wouldn't be here without you

3.

healing produces second chances
put down your burdens
welcome tests of courage
collective successes
are always possible

offer inspiration
you are the star
you are the fool
you are a source of powerful
intuition connections
pointing you in directions
along paths that keep opening

leave convention to them
your open heart is not stilted
your dreams, vivid
territories unexplored are yours
the stories will be different from theirs

it is not caution you are throwing
but dead weight
you are saved
for things greater
remember
to say thank you
we are holy
and sort of important

Candle Light Inspirations

1.

a strong sun of courage
is crossing your open heart
you feel warm affections
cold cleansed by inspirations
you are courageous enough
to know yourself
this is life's test
failure looks like struggle
but it is only a brief phase
you can swiftly shift perspectives
hope is just a word
it doesn't pay you at the end of the day
planets and stars and hard work

while your gut speaks caution
you see the horizon
tea cups overflowing with promise
balloons once weighted
are released and lightness
shines all over you
shared through you to kin
like being in love with everything
like looking out to a world, new

2.

one cannot chase balance
it must come to you
it is unexpected gifts
asking nothing in return
you deserve who you are
you are
not who you used to be
don't believe it
though expectations pile up
and morph into neglected resolve
there are so many more
dreams to follow
plenty more lessons
and yearnings to tame

the quiet ego
is the goal
do not poke holes
in your own convictions
do not do the anxiety dance
around your own knowing
get on the train
goddam drive the thing
and don't get off
till you've reached your destination

3.

change every now and then
take your freedom and your friends
lure luck your way
act aloof spin the wheel
and look away
the tea reader tells you
your tomorrows look good
but you don't believe her
the love you felt
had wings and lifted you away

that heart of yours
never felt trouble again
it grows and skips
excitements reproduced in pigments
and words and lens
blessed
say it again

Change

buried bones
to step lightly, respectfully
as if they don't already
know

we share quiet time
specially crafted
our conduct is
half and half known
we grow each time
we remember
visitor ancestors
anything but false humility
on special occasions
infrequently

when fire turns to ash
we hold hands
briefly releasing
family remains
places described as
sacred and hallowed
atoms and molecules
airborne wishes
granted at last

transformation is individual
elevation effected by
change
we are changing
without looking
we are changed

Coming Back

in the face of my father
as ten year old boy
she sees my sister
I continue to hold the picture
until she gets it
she doesn't so I tell her
that's the man from whom you bore
two children, sisters
the man long gone
and one sister gone too
he stood at the doorway
just behind the screen
peering out at the camera
knowing this is how he gets seen
his father, proud brown and robust
poses work ready in uniform
that takes him back and forth
along canada's tracks
each day retracing the journey
he does this for family
for the little boy at the door
and his brother
first cousin shares photos
they come from her mother
we share grandparents
our histories, twinned
that little boy as man
would spawn five of his own
and his brother, my uncle
had six
we are not broken
but disconnected
coming back
to remembering

Addicted

Addicted to freedom
Addicted to happiness
Addicted to empowerment
Addicted to music
Addicted to movement
Addicted to sobriety
Addicted to swimming pools
Addicted to groovy things
Addicted to the pen
Addicted to making radio
Addicted to gratitude
Addicted to the rhythm
Addicted to the beat
Addicted to breathing ocean air
Addicted to dancing
Addicted to singing
Addicted to sleep dreams
Addicted to the night skies
Addicted to heat
Addicted to brown skin
Addicted to thinking things through
Addicted to chill'n
Addicted to keeping my word
Addicted to telling the truth
Addicted to being reliable
Addicted to nationhood
Addicted to creation
Addicted to reactivating culture
Addicted to being fascinated
Addicted to being child-free
Addicted to letting shit go
Addicted to speaking up
Addicted to the source

Addicted to embracing my age
Addicted to female energies
Addicted to bumble bees
Addicted to good trades
Addicted to cancelling my cable
Addicted to travel
Addicted to shutting up
Addicted to knowing the future
Addicted to spirit family
Addicted to human family
Addicted to extended family
Addicted to sexy shoes
Addicted to ol' school disco
Addicted to memories
Addicted to compliments
Addicted to cigars
Addicted to inspiration
Addicted to answers
Addicted to intelligence
Addicted to smudging
Addicted to touching trees
Addicted to black liquorice
Addicted to performance art
Addicted to a good cry
Addicted to keeping my distance
Addicted to civil disobedience
Addicted to toast and coffee
Addicted to hot baths
Addicted to fairy lights
Addicted to planning for tomorrow
Addicted to calling bullshit
Addicted to self-sufficiency
Addicted to smiling
Addicted to being punctual
Addicted to all things shiny

Addicted to hilarious laughter
Addicted to doing accents
Addicted to picking up after myself
Addicted to praying
Addicted to daylight
Addicted to intuition
Addicted to brown skin
Addicted to repeating myself
Addicted to choice
Addicted to choosing
Addicted to supporting
Addicted to working
Addicted to producing
Addicted to your attention
Addicted to silver not gold
Addicted to vegas baby!
Addicted to living

Six O'clock

nothing stops the throbbing
emanating from the bottom
of my feet my souls
opening with surprising ease
reconnecting to roots
of home, one home, rejoining
with perfect timing
a turned season
is as good as a blank calendar
this mourning takes so long
my feet are throbbing

the weatherman doesn't even have the language
to describe the damp bite of spring
strung along ocean breezes
travelling westward
on polluted clouds too heavy to sail past
too stubborn to purge
my hands swell on days like this
my hands stay hidden and I am mistaken
for homeless

I have returned to live briefly
with city cedars
I have returned to my place of birth
practicing stillness
I really love the silence
it amplifies all the sonic voices
ordinarily not heard

I am speaking to a man stuck between worlds
addressing him sideways
my once wandering heart has landed

while I wait for the rumbling
imagine towers tumbling
knowing mountains will remain
we think of our loved ones
over oceans and plains

sentimentality is a weakness
it works against us
the government calculates it
along with our taxes
emotional attachments control us
best not to want it
but we really can't help it

don't look at me too long
I don't like it
a lie is a long road
absent of intersections
limitations become routine
I am not immune to conditioning
what is it?
to reminisce is to take a vacation
with your former self
seeing again from perfect vantage points
taking notes for next time

when you live in a house
with the ghost of a pedophile
you keep doors closed
you learn to make deals
concentration comes at a cost
the birds sing at six o'clock
the same time my dreams stop

Strong Dark Coffee

loose tobacco
tight cigarettes
stimulants
thick smoky suggestions
the poets are happy
at the ocean
the writers mope
in the rain
are we being
too supportive
of the same ol' shit
the youth are digging deep
reinvigorate sixty's rhetoric
what is learned behaviour
and what is politics?

I am telling you
we know nothing
but collectively
we can figure it out

think
he said
don't believe it
had to say it twice
to adopt it
where there's a will
there's a website
that time between thinking
and knowing is poetry
creative hangovers and caffeine
just make the coffee stronger
please

NDNs on the Airwaves

that's what radio is
it is air and electricity
with sounds reflective of us

don't like it tune it out
trust it, turn it up
keep listening
tune out the static
it doesn't represent us

voice is the music
music is information
sounds touch our lands
with answers, healing
colonial disturbance in the force
those powerful two-way signals
brought me home
providing a new family
a brother Two-Bears
and all the musicians
gathering round the radio
giving and receiving
their voices
our voices
new breath

keeping the language alive
revving up wattage
sending signals farther
over rivers
across corn fields
into homes and halls
community bingo calls

keeping the signal pulsating
vibrating with voice
want to know what's going on
turn on the radio

we all just want
to have our say
we want
home
to be part of the soundscape
landscape
I just wanted you
to hear me
coming home
sending signals
long distance
arrows piercing centre

sound waves
and voices
old old voices
you know those voices
(being called back)
rivers, these are the veins
where life recedes, receives
our people
they leave
it doesn't happen to make any sense
reach through time
electricity travels past currents
carrying news and memories
(sometimes the spirit arrives ahead of time)
oration as powerful as actions
open, receive these gifts

these rapid sound waves
flowing, over flowing
flooding
bringing you, bringing me
bringing us
blues
(when I think of home, I think of the circular journey)
speaking to you, speaking to me
speaking to us
in languages without...

crossing cultures
bringing sending
staying on the land
informing and defining

this
is radio

I've been here
all the time

Faces

where do we get these faces
obvious faces
full of history
time's canvas
life and light
memory catchers
relation faces
no choices to choose
we have no more need
to ride horses
yet we still ride horses
these expressions
of traditions
evade critical
examinations
why do we still do it
this way

our anchors
get lighter
with age
and relations
relation faces
fade
where do the new faces
when do they arrive
listen for your frequency
for prophetical lyrics
rich affirmations
wisdom is infinite
how close are we willing
to get to our own questions

channelled responses
without knowing
yet knowing all the same
flying over velvet landscapes
through vaporous whiteness
air as light as air
acknowledge earth's superiority
over everything

we hold important
moments albeit fleeting
moments fleeting
meeting with these
cumbersome faces
using muscles and emotions
control and ego to convey
simple meaning
I am bringing my brown face
to yours together we join
our thoughts
speak nothing of what the other
may be thinking
just knowing it is
bigger than us
it is our ticket
we line up
opposite each other
leave room for
immense respect
watch trust walk in
read the lines between us
facing sentences
a lifetime of this

Singing the Peace Hymn

Ocean and Shore

we met in a wet dream
gliding along weightless
we met in a time
when trust wavered
confidence feigned
I waited and waded
each night to see you
thinking back
I could smell you
pungent effervescent decay
musky mix of day
witness tides
rise and relax
I react to you
pull me close you
wanted me
to see myself
fearful of reflection
I breathe when you breathe
we are both
ocean and shore
matter and magic
I want to stir you
into every syllable
and speak
chant
no hum
your thunder waves
your original name
reclaim our bodies together
un-pollute our histories
and give you back yourself
as you have done
for me

Belly of the Mother

did the queen teach
her son (grand)sons
dignity
why is she
still calling me
subject
I offer
intelligent experience
and humble jewellery
expected to be taken
seriously
because the only trick
tucked up my sleeve
is family

we bring
arrowheads and ink
food and fake booze
we like the patterns of industrialization
the clouds are cool
but never do we trust
the track of their thinking
or tradition or roots
we have GPS positioning
future versions of ourselves
will come calling
call it making
reservations

he says:
you have to find yourself
he says:
he likes her succulence

the outer shell
of a woman's power is
protection
when penetrated
we are gifted
complex beauty
she chooses
which secrets to serve
dish with one spoon
no language for feelings
no language for movements
no branding practices
made of hashtags
only salty coffee
emotions running raw as sobriety
find your footing
get used to it
pay attention to what
you're sensing
trust it
who are the
the Indians
what are they saying
we are representing
confused
traditions

has the over-saturation
of images
left us faceless
like the medicine doll
in love with her own reflection
ego taking over ego taking
quite the beating
hello from london
wondering

how'd SHE do it?
my magic is stilted
my mouth not saying
my meaning
I am hearing
them speaking
trying to keep from jumping
but trying is not doing

don't trust the corn
don't eat the watermelon
resist all the wonderful fashions
stop calculating the exchange
look both ways
we are in the belly
of the mother
who has gorged
on us before

The London Cocktail

the london cocktail
is one part smoke
two parts honey
three parts hairspray
four parts tourism

being playful
about important issues
is serious work
material and meaning
medium and messaging
listening for ghost notes
in overheated underground crowds
swelling sounds so emotional
they send you over(every)time

her majesty's people are crawling
all over her
enamoured with war ships moored
right in the middle of the river
call and response
call
respond
bing boing
bing bong
boing

cameras capturing subjects
350 times per day
we arrived thirsty and dirty
ready to be astonished
by opulence
instead we see dreams

of industriousness
ancestor legacies
fixated on making a living
identical row housing
and working
on happiness

it's July 1st
and margaret atwood
is pleased to see
everyone dressed
as handmaids in the square
while she, the closest
thing to royalty
explains poetry
over tea and cake
served by migrants
at canada house

in the future
there will be Mohawks
we left them gifts
to find using co-ordinates
the architects of this game
want to connect
with three time frames
at once

I watch for smoke
from terra cotta chimneys
signals that will tell me
but those fires
are never lit
and that smoke
never comes

Hot Oceans

monochrome
does not come from here
and there is no such thing
as silence
earth speaks
in creature voice
in critter voice
sky languages
violent and wild
(ocean) breaths
human echoes
territories remember
history horrors
honest earth
people earth people
living rocks
on wind-whipped
and rust bent tundra
sand skins
warm, hot
HHHHHOT
no silence
no cold
no richness
no sadness
no choice
no stillness
salt and rock
north of south
beautiful tones
linger on the land
salt of the earth
birthed in
hot oceans

Suspended

silent as soil
the value of stillness
divided
consciousness
existence suspended
suspension
blending
in
with
as
I am
I am
not
I am
the infinite
horizon
from where
sits
tomorrows' tomorrow
emotional voices
hearing hearts
he-ear he-ear he-ear
footprints
echoes
following songs
inside I am
growing oceans

timeless
anxious
endless suspension

come get me, no leave me

I am content
earth has me
universe, tomorrow
tomorrow's mystery
and so it goes
and so it goes
and so it goes

Croxxing

a forever bridge
tender-footed
curious
cautious
respectfully
entering
abandoning
one side
introducing
all of us
we are
bringing
customs
protocols
to the other
over
we go
over
to the other
protocols
customs
bringing
we are
all of us
introducing
one side
abandoning
entering
respectfully
cautious
curious
tender-footed
a forever bridge
croxxing

Salt of the Land

aguila ghost winds
trio of boatmen
salt spiced shadows
speechless heat screaming

rocks in the head
ageless lifespan
takes you too soon
falling over cliffs
into ocean crevasse
200 years is ancient
he is waiting
shoeless stillness
to be leader
expert in why
the shadows stay
stunning (she) shy beauty
so brave
duty to her people
un-touched, raped all the same
the miners hands change
nothing, nothing changed
checking for exists
born leaning into winds
soft spoken speeches
on roadless sand land
no work, no eat

beach fish cleaning
today´s catch
tomorrow dreaming
fifty kite-surfers
dancing in unison

when wind is friend
the one-eyed lady
looks, she sees them coming
she sees them leaving
Inukshuk symbols of themselves
she watches everything
she washes everything
all day long laundry
passed down from generations
no elders
no elders

but direct t.v.
inconsistent signal
not enough for answers
to take root
no sense of time

best friends blinking
high noon drinking
under the shadow of boats
telling jokes
in hand-made hammocks
baby-man rides his whale
to shore packing tall tales
from re-generated oceans
two dynamic forces
making lighting
in vapid villages
chasing everything
La Patrona
will take your money
she will build your house
out of coral and sea shells
she will tell you salt is spiritual

and leave you
to make up your own mind
he hides
in his brothers shadow
waits eight long months
for the next rain
breathing salt
wearing the sea

this is not the land
of the coconuts
and coffee
it is a forever
home

House of Stories

the house is never empty
writers pack inspiration
the ones blessed and chosen
Joy, of writing
looking south
at her cherry tree
and all the birds visiting

Mohawk medicine is placed
at four corners
residents speak
to left over energies
panting without running
stomach pebbles
she tells her it is he
the broken pieces of a man
looking for solace
trapped inside his own
grief, gone
and yet so present

safety practices
in effect
first stop
in a new phase
working the research
like a genealogist
difference being
she goes to the source
to the people themselves

upon territory
where displacement
never took up residence
bringing them offerings
ancestral relations revisiting

the northern facing headboard
inspires dreams of singers
this closeness is telling her something
a moment of melancholy
when passing brick buildings
she was born of a sad beginning
leading
to a house
of poems

Into out of the Woods

earth shows us
she is still young
gases rising
flying off
in all six directions
not reckless but careless
she can't help it
can't help it
one bit
this is pre-racial
post ice-age
expressions in
vaporous residue
the people   see
the people   move
land has natural valleys
where spirits pass
into and out
ancient walls
miles high
hidden doors
portals for passage
she knows this
saw this too
minds stretched
in expansive
comprehensions

these visions   I get it

surpassing limits
weaving through forests
towards advancements

she asked
if I wanted to keep going

I said
I already am

the road
behind with distance
grows
she knows this
she saw this too
sees it now
she was first
first to lead search parties
research we call it
finding
never discovering
the people   see
the people   move
mountain crests point
up there   we say
where
technology wants this
so bad   it rattles
no way to take it
but you can buy air
shake shake shakespear
knows the sound of
shhhhhh, shhhhhh,
and shhhhhh

swallowing air
gallons of it
breathing green
acres of it
looking out

to speak
from a place
of absolute truth
free of metaphor
and hyperbole
detecting rock writing
relevant and meaningful
realizing it's not war at all
but ill conceived theatre
and reality t.v.
it has nothing
nothing to do with dreams
no dreams I've seen
sacred is different
than secret
supported existence
on another plane
up there
the mountain points
up there

immovable and beautiful
constant witnesses
these are our cathedrals
standing free - a kind of freedom
leaving me breathless
thin air stillness
majestic with unidentified
inhabitants

yes   she says yes

Indigenous birds surrender themselves
on mountain sides so they can speak
to us in dreams
the language of symbols and feelings

we dare to stand eye to eye
with these giants
must we conquer
all the mysteries
and dissect romance from it
it is enough to gaze
in silent amazement
I asked her
how does she do it
she said
it's just there

the dancers
have been here
and with any luck
they'll come again
to teach us and interpret
what the river
is saying
most sounds
are not man-made noise
they are voices
constantly talking
this awe never fades
many times my tobacco
has been placed
and the tiny piles dot the woods
the mountains carry their prayers
this is trust
call it faith
it is food
our spirits crave
up there
the mountain crests
point us
up there

Born (Again) Savage

make no offering
take none too
enter the enemy's home
boldly show
who I am
when they reach
to control anything
of me
I remember
to fly
places of their making
taking
their brightest boy
between my legs
he hesitates
remembering
he too can deny
illogical teachings
he too
can make human mistakes
and survive
in the middle
I see all
the silver
collected from
before
not tempted
because I remember
I fly
to summits
of famous mountains
you must remember you
too

A Bullet You Can't Call Back

origin stories of dispossession
become rotten foundations
where generations multiply themselves
in fictitious histories
tell me your story
don't tell me mine
stop pause
don't say anything at all
sit with what you know

please
stop saying
decolonial love
to describe an identity
you intend to be
too many buzz words
weaken efficiency
of languages in recovery
don't be part of the problem

the beast has turned inward
outings to movies, to churches
schools and music shows
are never guaranteed safe return
whose dark manifestations are these
inhumane is not a normal state
it is not us
this, is us

time spent in reactive and protective defence
leaves little room for new inspirations
ask for assistance
assistance will come

who are the new gunslingers
who are they taking orders from
a bullet travels faster
than the word no
this is terror
ripping through visions
I hear you
don't make me
tell you again
honour me
don't make me beg

what happened to generosity
what happened to originality

words are powerful energy
but they do not stand on their own
saying something is something
does not make it so
use sound
work the verbs

show me respect
I'll take that bullet in the chest
and turn the gun on you too
I am doing my best
staying human
how about you

No Place

space and light
a way to communicate
wait
beginnings again
before
fire creation story
noise
antennas reaching
existence
mysterious
flag-less landscape
it happens here
interior
going inside
birth of possibilities
fleeting
accepting
unknown emotions
blowing ash
into intelligence
blow it
thoughts as natural
as dead centre silence

silence as inspiring as
sound matter memory
place me with family
inside cultural tombs
discussions heal wounds
make amends
it is all possible

No More Birthdays

I have a sister
"Yes"
still with us
her murderous end
so thoughtless
we are survivors
we live
as one half of the other
know our stories
look together after
a broken-hearted mother
she once older
I am now elder
no more birthdays
only anniversaries of the day
we remain challenged
by forgiveness
obsessed with this healing
she travels
with our ancestors
constantly showing us
ways to live stronger

"Yes, I have a Sister."
she is with me everyday

Good Trades

I hold you in my mouth
sensual medicine
worked and served
with instinct
I am making
good trades

is it enough to offer
milk and bones
a bouquet of roses
grown on the grave of
your grandmother?
I will separate your name
tattooed on my thigh
and offer yourself
back to you

I'll make these trades
all day long with you
how about this
I perform a skit
where I play
both girl and boy
protagonist and villain
I'll wear your mask
you wear mine
so we can make love
to ourselves and each other
at the same time

what if I write you a poem
wait never mind

our love is defined
as blended blood
high-bred-romantic
we are thoroughbreds
with strong swift limbs
if you run I run after you
catch you wrestle you
in Mohawk-mock struggle

we are star attractions
centre ring circus
bring your cousins
we accept trades

Far Away Fires

coming together
runners, charting
new courses
and stories
People of the Shirt
the original band
on the run
it was done
remembering
that comes
from knowing
the strong hold
holding ground
perhaps
those fires
wanted to be
united
needed to be
together
keep burning

it was never about
blood thinning
but blending
over time
we became kin
married in
leaders
language
habitual land
defending together
allies
no choice
but to pick a side

history
records the win
what of the women
navigating their place
new dynamics constructed
from disrupted traditions
how many nations
and generations
cycle through
before choices
enacted again